States

WEST VIRGINIA

by Bridget Parker

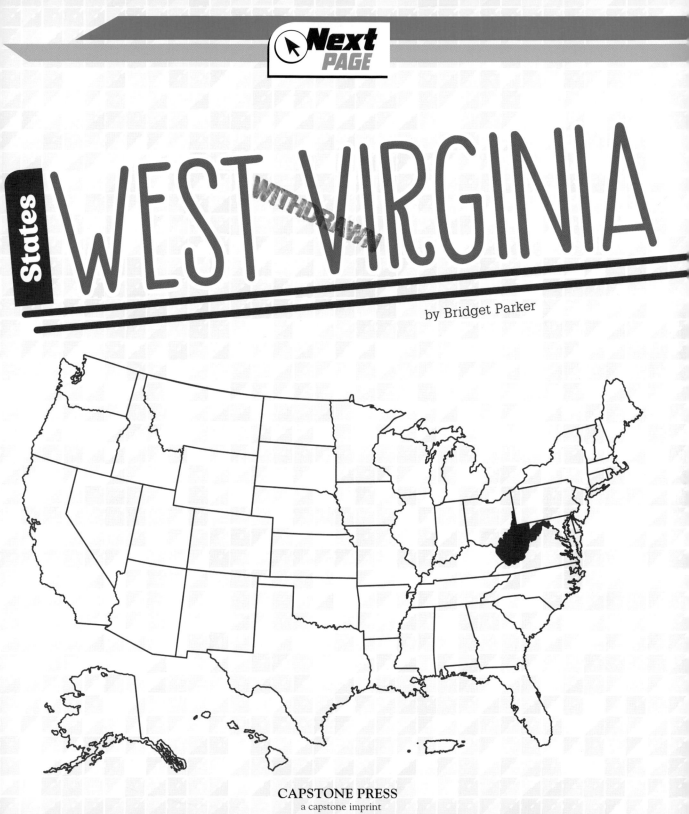

CAPSTONE PRESS
a capstone imprint

Next Page Books are published by Capstone Press,
1710 Roe Crest Drive, North Mankato, Minnesota 56003
www.mycapstone.com

Library of Congress Cataloging-in-Publication Data
Cataloging-in-publication information is on file with the Library of
Congress.
ISBN 978-1-5157-0437-9 (library binding)
ISBN 978-1-5157-0496-6 (paperback)
ISBN 978-1-5157-0548-2 (ebook PDF)

Editorial Credits
Jaclyn Jaycox, editor; Kazuko Collins and Katy LaVigne, designers;
Morgan Walters, media researcher; Tori Abraham, production specialist

Photo Credits
Alamy: Niday Picture Library, 27, PF-(usna), 12; Capstone Press:
Angie Gahler, map 4, 7; CriaImages.com: Jay Robert Nash Collection,
top 19; Dreamstime: Jerry Coli, top 18; Library of Congress: Prints
and Photographs Division Washington, D.C., 28; Newscom: Everett
Collection, middle 18, Glasshouse Images, 25, Jim West imageBROKER,
29; One Mile Up, Inc., flag, seal 23; Shutterstock: abutyrin, 14,
Aspen Photo, 16, branislavpudar, bottom 24, Connie Barr, bottom
left 20, Daniel Prudek, bottom left 21, Everett Historical, 26, Helga
Esteb, middle 19, hramovnick, top 24, igzag Mountain Art, bottom
right 20, Jason Patrick Ross, top right 21, Jeff Feverston, bottom
right 21, Jon Bilous, cover, 7, bottom left 8, 9, Katherine Welles, 5,
Kenneth Keifer, 6, Lissandra Melo, 17, Malachi Jacobs, bottom right
8, MarkVanDykePhotography, 10, mextrix, top right 20, mimo, 15,
Todd Taulman, 13, Tom Reichner, top left 21, Zamada, top left 20; U.S.
Air Force photo, bottom 18; Wikimedia: ForestWander, 11, Senate.gov,
bottom 19

All design elements by Shutterstock

Printed and bound in China.
0316/CA21600187
012016   009436F16

TABLE OF CONTENTS

Want to take your research further? Ask your librarian if your school subscribes to PebbleGo Next. If so, when you see this helpful symbol ⬀ throughout the book, log onto www.pebblegonext.com for bonus downloads and information.

LOCATION

West Virginia is a southeastern state. It is the only state that lies completely within the Appalachian Mountains. Virginia lies along its eastern and southern borders. Kentucky and Ohio are to the west. Pennsylvania and Maryland border West Virginia to the north. West Virginia's capital, Charleston, is also the state's largest city. Huntington and Parkersburg are its next two largest cities.

PebbleGo Next Bonus!
To print and label your own map, go to www.pebblegonext.com and search keywords:
WV MAP

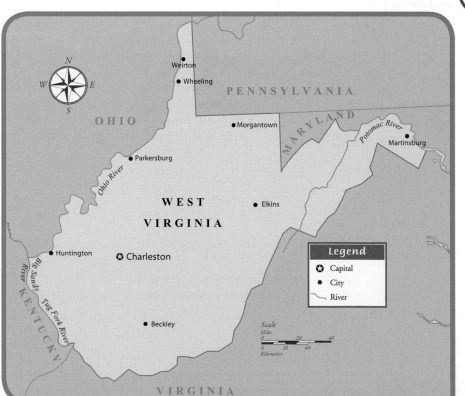

The population of Charleston is about 51,000 people.

GEOGRAPHY

West Virginia is one of the country's most rugged states. Rolling hills cover the western part of the state. The Appalachian Plateau covers most of this area. West Virginia's eastern and central parts are mountainous. Eastern West Virginia lies within the heavily forested Appalachian Ridge and Valley region. The Allegheny Mountains divide the Appalachian Plateau from the Ridge and Valley region. They include West Virginia's highest point, Spruce Knob. It is 4,861 feet (1,482 meters) above sea level. The Blue Ridge region is at the state's eastern tip. The Blue Ridge Mountains are in this region.

PebbleGo Next Bonus! To watch a video about Harpers Ferry National Historical Park, go to www.pebblegonext.com and search keywords: **WV VIDEO**

Dunloup Falls is one of the many creeks that flows into the New River Gorge.

The trees on Spruce Knob only grow branches on one side due to the harsh winds and weather conditions.

Legend

▲ Highest Point

🏔 Mountain Range

⬛ National Historical Park

〰 River

N
W E
S

Potomac River

Harpers Ferry National Historical Park

BLUE RIDGE

Ohio River

APPALACHIAN RIDGE AND VALLEY

BLUE RIDGE MOUNTAINS

Spruce Knob ▲

Shenandoah River

APPALACHIAN PLATEAU

Kanawha River

Big Sandy River

ALLEGHENY MOUNTAINS

Tug Fork River

APPALACHIAN MOUNTAINS

Scale
Miles
0   20   40
0   20   40
Kilometers

WEATHER

West Virginia's average temperatures are 72 degrees Fahrenheit (22 degrees Celsius) during summer and 33°F (1°C) during winter. Temperatures usually are cooler in the mountains and warmer in the valleys.

Average High and Low Temperatures (Charleston, WV)

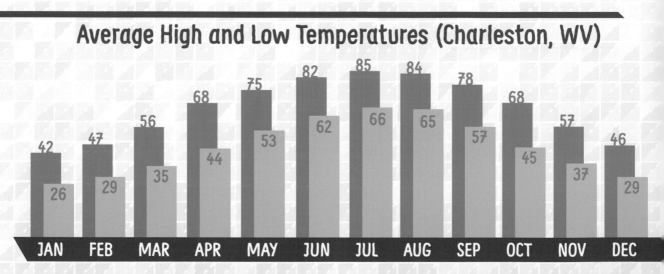

	JAN	FEB	MAR	APR	MAY	JUN	JUL	AUG	SEP	OCT	NOV	DEC
High	42	47	56	68	75	82	85	84	78	68	57	46
Low	26	29	35	44	53	62	66	65	57	45	37	29

New River Gorge Bridge

This steel arch bridge spans 3,030 feet (924 m) over the New River Gorge near Fayetteville. The bridge is 876 feet (267 m) above the New River, making it the third-highest bridge in the country. The third Saturday of October is Bridge Day. During this festival, people are allowed to parachute off the bridge into the gorge below.

Harpers Ferry National Historical Park

About a half million people visit the historic town of Harpers Ferry each year. Museums help visitors learn about life in the 19th century in this scenic town, which was also the location of John Brown's raid on a federal armory in 1859.

Seneca Caverns

Visitors can enjoy a caving adventure at Seneca Caverns and Stratosphere Cave. The limestone caves formed millions of years ago and contain unique geological formations.

HISTORY AND GOVERNMENT

Union soldiers from the 22nd New York State Militia camp near Harpers Ferry during the Civil War.

England established its Virginia colony in 1607. After the Revolutionary War (1775–1783), western and eastern Virginians felt differently about slavery. Most easterners supported slavery. Some western Virginians disagreed with it. In 1861 the Civil War (1861–1865) began after some southern states seceded from, or left, the United States, including Virginia. The western counties voted to stay with the Union. Five days after the Civil War began, western Virginia voted to secede from the state. On June 20, 1863, West Virginia became the 35th state.

West Virginia's government is divided into three branches. The legislative branch makes the state laws. It includes the 34-member Senate and the 100-member House of Delegates. The executive branch carries out the state's laws and is led by the governor. The judicial branch is made up of judges and their courts. They interpret the state's laws.

The dome of West Virginia's capitol building stands taller than the dome of the Capitol in Washington, D.C.

INDUSTRY

Tourism is West Virginia's leading industry. Visitors hike in the state's forests and parks. Rock climbers explore West Virginia's mountains. Whitewater rafters float down West Virginia's fast-flowing rivers.

Coal is one of West Virginia's greatest natural resources. West Virginia produces about 15 percent of the country's coal and almost half of the coal that the United States sells to other countries. West Virginia also produces salt, natural gas, and oil. Most of the state's salt is used to make chlorine. Chlorine is a chemical used in some cleaning supplies and to make plastic and other materials.

Of the 55 counties in West Virginia, there are only two that do not have coal.

Another major natural resource in West Virginia is forestry. The state's oak and cherry trees are used for lumber.

The forestry industry employs over 30,000 people in West Virginia.

POPULATION

Most West Virginians live in rural areas. West Virginia's largest cities are small compared to the largest cities in many other states. Most West Virginians have European backgrounds. The first settlers who came to West Virginia were German, English, Welsh, and Scottish. Other Europeans, including Russians, Hungarians, Italians, and Poles, came after the Civil War. Many of these people came to work at the state's railroad companies, coal mines, and logging camps. Few minorities live in West Virginia. African-Americans make up only about 3 percent of the state's population. Only about 1 percent of the state's residents are Hispanic, and less than 1 percent are Asian.

Population by Ethnicity

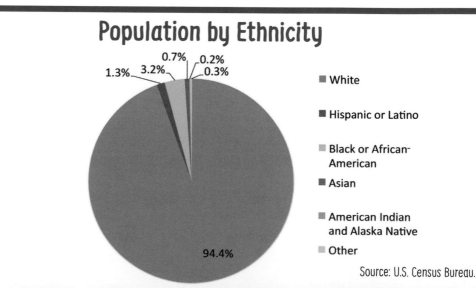

1.3% 3.2% 0.7% 0.2% 0.3%

94.4%

- White
- Hispanic or Latino
- Black or African-American
- Asian
- American Indian and Alaska Native
- Other

Source: U.S. Census Bureau.

FAMOUS PEOPLE

Mary Lou Retton (1968–) won the gold medal for gymnastics in the 1984 Olympic Games. In 1997 she was inducted into the International Gymnastics Hall of Fame. She was born in Fairmont.

Booker T. Washington (1856–1915) founded Alabama's Tuskegee Institute, now known as Tuskegee University, for African-Americans. He was born in Virginia and grew up in West Virginia.

Chuck Yeager (1923–) is a retired Air Force test pilot and general. In 1947 he became the first human to fly faster than the speed of sound. He was born in Myra.

Pearl Buck (1892–1973) was a writer. She is best known for the novel *The Good Earth*. Buck won the 1938 Nobel Prize for literature. She was born in Hillsboro.

Brad Paisley (1972–) is a Grammy Award–winning country music singer and songwriter. His albums have sold millions of copies. He was born in Glen Dale.

John D. (Jay) Rockefeller IV (1937–) served as governor (1977–1985) and as U.S. senator (1985–2014) from West Virginia. He was born in New York.

STATE SYMBOLS

sugar maple

rhododendron

cardinal

golden delicious apple

Animal

black bear

Butterfly

monarch butterfly

Insect

honeybee

Fish

brook trout

PebbleGo Next Bonus! To make a dessert using ingredients
that come from trees found in West Virginia, go to
www.pebblegonext.com and search keywords:

WV RECIPE

FAST FACTS

STATEHOOD
1863

CAPITAL ☆
Charleston

LARGEST CITY •
Charleston

SIZE
24,038 square miles (62,258 square kilometers) land area
(2010 U.S. Census Bureau)

POPULATION
1,854,304 (2013 U.S. Census estimate)

STATE NICKNAME
Mountain State, Panhandle State

STATE MOTTO
"Montani semper liberi," a Latin phrase that means
"Mountaineers are always free"

STATE SEAL

The state seal features a farmer and a miner standing next to a rock. The farmer represents agriculture and the miner represents industry. West Virginia's date of statehood, June 20, 1863, is on the rock. Rifles are near the seal's bottom. The Cap of Liberty, a symbol of freedom, lies on top of the rifles. The state motto, "Montani semper liberi," is written under the rifles. It means "Mountaineers are always free."

PebbleGo Next Bonus! To print and color your own flag, go to www.pebblegonext.com and search keywords: **WV FLAG**

STATE FLAG

West Virginia's state flag was adopted in 1929. The image from the state seal is featured on a white background. On the seal, a farmer and a miner stand next to a rock. The farmer represents agriculture and the miner represents industry. The rhododendron, the state flower, surrounds the seal. A blue border surrounds the flag.

MINING PRODUCTS

coal, natural gas, petroleum, limestone

MANUFACTURED GOODS

chemicals, metal products, petroleum and coal products

FARM PRODUCTS

cattle, corn, wheat, soybeans

PebbleGo Next Bonus!
To learn the lyrics to
the state song, go to
www.pebblegonext.com
and search keywords:

WU SONG

WEST VIRGINIA TIMELINE

1607 — England establishes the Virginia colony.

1620 — The Pilgrims establish a colony in the New World in present-day Massachusetts.

1671 — Englishmen Thomas Batts and Robert Fallam travel to southern West Virginia.

1731 — Welshman Morgan Morgan establishes the first settlement in present-day West Virginia near Bunker Hill.

1754–1763 — Many of the battles of the French and Indian War take place in West Virginia.

 **1783** The American colonies win independence from Great Britain in the Revolutionary War (1775–1783).

 **1815** Natural gas is discovered near Charleston.

1859 On October 16 abolitionist John Brown and a group of men raid a federal armory in Harpers Ferry; this raid increases tension between pro-slavery and anti-slavery activists.

 **1861–1865** The Union and the Confederacy fight the Civil War.

On October 24 western Virginia counties separate from Virginia and form a government that supports the Union in the Civil War.

1863 West Virginia becomes the 35th state on June 20.

1885 Charleston becomes the permanent state capital.

1907 At least 360 people die in a coal mine explosion on December 6 in Monongah, making it the worst coal mine disaster in U.S. history.

1914–1918 World War I is fought; the United States enters the war in 1917.

1920–1921

Disputes between miners and coal mine operators cause violence to break out in what becomes known as the West Virginia Coal Wars.

1921

West Virginia becomes the first state to charge a sales tax.

1939–1945

World War II is fought; the United States enters the war in 1941.

1968

On November 20, 78 people die in a coal mine disaster in Farmington.

1977

The New River Gorge Bridge opens near Fayetteville on October 22. At the time, it was the world's longest steel-arch bridge.

2002 A major flood in May causes major damage to southern West Virginia.

2010 On April 5 an explosion at the Massey Energy company mine kills 29 miners.

2014 In January chemicals from a coal processing plant leak into the Elk River, making the drinking water unsafe in Charleston.

2015 Researchers at West Virginia University uncover vehicle emission data that leads to $18 billion in fines for Volkswagon.

Glossary

abolitionist *(ab-uh-LI-shuhn-ist)*—a person who worked to end slavery

census *(SEN-Suhss)*—an official count of all the people living in a country or district

executive *(ig-ZE-kyuh-tiv)*—the branch of government that makes sure laws are followed

gorge *(GORJ)*—a canyon with steep walls that rise straight upward

industry *(IN-duh-stree)*—a business which produces a product or provides a service

judicial *(joo-DISH-uhl)*—to do with the branch of government that explains and interprets the laws

legislature *(LEJ-iss-lay-chur)*—a group of elected officials who have the power to make or change laws for a country or state

petroleum *(puh-TROH-lee-uhm)*—an oily liquid found below the earth's surface used to make gasoline, heating oil, and many other products

raid *(RAYD)*—a sudden, surprise attack on a place

secede *(si-SEED)*—to formally withdraw from a group or an organization, often to form another organization

tourism *(TOOR-i-zuhm)*—the business of taking care of visitors to a country or place

Read More

Dillard, Sheri. *What's Great About West Virginia?* Our Great States. Minneapolis: Lerner Publications, 2016.

Ganeri, Anita. *United States of America: A Benjamin Blog and His Inquisitive Dog Guide.* Country Guides. Chicago: Heinemann Raintree, 2015.

Petreycik, Rick. *West Virginia.* It's My State! New York: Cavendish Square Publishing, 2014.

Internet Sites

FactHound offers a safe, fun way to find Internet sites related to this book. All of the sites on FactHound have been researched by our staff.

Here's all you do:

Visit *www.facthound.com*

Type in this code: 9781515704379

 Check out projects, games and lots more at **www.capstonekids.com**

Critical Thinking Using the Common Core

1. Take a look at the map on page 7. What river runs along the northwest border of West Virginia? (Craft and Structure)

2. When did West Virginia become a state? (Key Ideas and Details)

3. West Virginia produces how much of the country's coal? (Key Ideas and Details)

Index